MW00966497

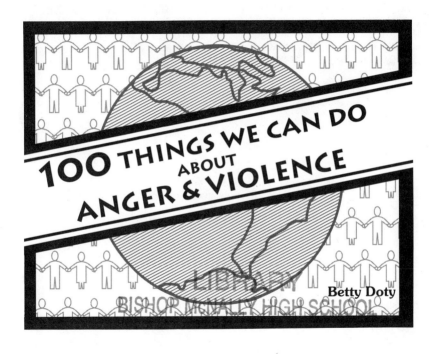

100 THINGS WE CAN DO ABOUT ANGER & VIOLENCE

ABOUT

Betty Doty

Other books by Betty Doty - GETTING THROUGH TO OTHERS WITHOUT ANGER, SHAKE THE ANGER HABIT! (with Pat Rooney), THE ANGER PUZZLE (with Pat Rooney), BREAK THE ANGER TRAP, MARRIAGE INSURANCE, PUBLISH YOUR OWN HANDBOUND BOOKS, and HEY LOOK...I MADE A BOOK! (with Rebecca Meredith). The Bookery, 6899 Riata Drive, Redding, CA 96002-9786.

```
Doty, Betty.
    100 things we can do about anger & violence / Betty Doty.
        p.    cm.
    ISBN 0-930822-18-8 (alk. paper) : $9.95
    1. Anger--Miscellanea.  2. Violence--Miscellanea.  3. Adjustment
(Psychology)--Miscellanea.    I. Title.   II. Title: One hundred
things we can do about anger and violence.
BF575.A5D68   1994
152.4'7--dc20
                                                        93-40615
                                                          CIP
```

Congratulations! You've been able to pick up this book!

Obviously you're not so alarmed about escalating anger and violence that you've got your head hidden in the sand… **at least for this minute.**

Step 1 (toward finding more of what you can do about anger and violence): You can recognize that you've already taken a first step by reading this first page. (That was easy, wasn't it?)

I don't think any of us hide our heads in the sand except for one reason: We feel totally helpless to find a better alternative.

What you'll be discovering here is an exciting alternative to head-hiding.

Step 2: At this point, your part is merely to settle down to read. You know you can always retreat if you need to. But you can also brush the sand out of your eyes again and again... and return each time to more reading.

My urgency to write comes from what I see inside my own family counseling room. It's a **pattern of thinking** which **inevitably** leads to anger and violence, a kind of thinking which creates what I call an anger/power-struggle trap.

And I've found that this trap can be broken.

Step 3: I wish I could tell you **instantly** how the trap can be broken, and how to take **100 dramatic steps** which will guarantee success. Instead, these are little steps, some as small as answering a too-easy question. But you may be surprised… and very pleased… to find where the steps lead.

As a counselor I've found that I can't assume, ever, that I know exactly what will work for any one person. All I can do, besides listen, is tell another person what works for me. **Then I'll generalize about a way of thinking which works for many others...** so they're not **forming** so much anger.

Step 4: I'm thinking now about the way learning occurs, and here's a question for you: What is it that makes the difference for you, **in the way a suggestion is given,** whether you can take that particular suggestion or not?

For each reader to actually find what works to help a person bring their **anger level** down, and also society's, **here's my best proposal.**

Step 5: It will help if you stop reading for a minute and identify at least **a little** of your own anger. (And it doesn't matter how you label it… maybe resentment, self-anger or full-blown rage.) Then you'll be in a position to make some guesses as to whether the suggestions in this book will work **for others…** as you'll soon be finding if they work for you.

Consider the implications for our society if you find that just one person, you, can actually get your anger level down by way of reading a book. Mind boggling? Yes. But this can actually happen, according to feedback I've gotten from earlier books: **SHAKE THE ANGER HABIT!** and **THE ANGER PUZZLE** (both co-authored with Pat Rooney), **BREAK THE ANGER TRAP** and **GETTING THROUGH TO OTHERS WITHOUT ANGER.**

Step 6: Why not let your mind be boggled for a while? Then you can let it settle down to **just a few of the implications** of a person's being able to reduce their own anger level… just by reading a book.

Here's one way of describing what I see in our society. It's as if we're surrounded by spreading brushfires of anger and violence. And unless we take more effective action, and soon, **we're in real danger of a firestorm... for which there's no defense.**

Step 7: What is it we can do to quench enough brushfires? Use different buckets?... or different water? Maybe you agree that we desperately need more creative thinking... and it may have to come from people **not too different from you and me**.

Avoiding helplessness is essential, as I believe that it's **helplessness** itself which breeds **anger.** And enough anger breeds **violence**… which feeds on itself. **The firestorm.**

Step 8: If it really is helplessness which triggers our own anger, we can become more alert to the factors which **guarantee** helplessness. For example, try asking different people to tell what's wrong with our society and notice their proposed corrections. If each person is talking about what **someone else ought to be doing,** you'll see the result of their talk: **more** despair and **more** helplessness and… **more** anger.

What happens if we truly believe that our society's gigantic problems, such as escalating anger and violence, can only be resolved by gigantic solutions... **and we won't be safe with each other** until we solve a long list of gigantic problems: injustice, prejudice, drug/alcohol abuse.........

Step 9: What would a society be like if this belief is widespread? Wouldn't we have what we have now, **many people nearly paralyzed with helplessness and fear?** Is it possible that we sense (rightly?) that **our current problem-solving methods** may not work fast enough to avoid approaching firestorms ?

When we recognize the importance of avoiding our own helplessness, at least we won't be spending precious time telling each other scare stories (maybe about such things as the dramatic increase in sales of bullet-proof vests for school children, for example).

Step 10: Instead of participating in helplessness talk, maybe you'll find that others want to discuss the ideas here (especially the one that's apparently the most ridiculous, **that people can actually learn to cut the anguish caused by their own anger… just by reading a book).**

#11

When a person comes in for counseling, I get a close view of the kind of thinking which creates helplessness… **and of the increasingly desperate actions which follow.** I hear how each person makes observations, defines problems and plans solutions. **Then it's as if I hear a trap closing and the thinking doubles back, again and again, to more helplessness.**

Step 11: Can you accept **the possibility** that our helplessness, both for individuals and our society, **may stem from the way we make observations and define problems… as that determines where we look for solutions?**

What would an individual be like who constantly feels **helpless...** and constantly engages in angry power struggles **in a futile attempt to dispel helplessness?** What would a society be like if it is composed of millions of such individuals? From my view of the individuals I see in such a trap, I reach this surprising conclusion: **Each person vows every day, and fails every day, to avoid getting angry and incurring others' anger.**

Step 12: Why do you think a person **ever** gets stuck in such a trap? And what kind of a mindset do you think would **guarantee** staying stuck? I'll be drawing more and more from the counseling room to see if we can find answers.

A person will tell me this: "But I've got to keep fighting or people would walk all over me... I'd be a nobody... If I give up I might as well be dead."

This trap, a power-struggle trap, tightens when we believe we have **no choice** except to fight or give up. Since giving up is unthinkable, the fighting has to go on and on... **even after we find that it isn't leading to success and good feelings.**

Step 13: In the counseling room, what do you think a counselor can do to **break the pattern of thinking** which traps us in angry power struggles?

We'll say a person **only** knows a problem-solving style based on win-lose power struggles. How can that person **ever** learn… **from their own experience…** that a win-win problem-solving style works better?

Step 14: I think this question merits your best thought. Unless we can find answers, I think we'll stay where we are: **trapped in incessant power struggles, grinding up each other and complaining about the resulting violence and our helplessness to make things better.**

#15

I think we desperately want to get the best out of each other... more often. But how? In the counseling room, when I see people move from a win-lose lifestyle to one of win-win, it's not easy to see exactly how it happens. I think it may begin with being accepted, exactly as they are, inside the counseling room. This seems to help each person become comfortable enough to talk and to listen. Then later, **if they choose**, they may decide to test some of the ideas which are generated.

Step 15: You can see that it's at least **possible** that each person's thinking **might** be juggled... and later it **might** settle down into a more comfortable pattern.

Seems to me that we all make our best decisions out of good feelings, when we're relaxed and comfortable, not when we're the most desperate. In order to enhance relaxation in the counseling room, I start by listening to each person... usually for two hours straight. My head's down in my notebook as I want to avoid giving any feedback at all.

Step 16: It's easy to see that accepting others makes it easier for them to be at their best with us... so here's your question: How is it that **we ourselves** can become more accepting? (I'll be giving my answers to that question in these pages.)

What I see in the counseling room is that each person is in a power struggle, whether with others or themselves. **They're focusing almost totally on what they're unable to get... and this keeps them continually wanting more help in order to get it... so they become nicer and nicer in order to get it... and when that doesn't work, they get angry and maybe meaner... and because of their anger they end up increasingly isolated... and more determined than ever to get what it is they haven't been able to get (which they believe will make things better).**

Step 17: Are you familiar with this pattern?

People in the counseling room tell me that they're unable to get through to others, and they mean that they can't persuade others to help them **enough**. The help they want may be vague or specific, and my summary is that they want others to **make their life easier.** (After a lifetime of such trying and failing to persuade others to help them **enough,** so their life will be easier, a person may eventually want to see the entire world destroyed as punishment for it's uncooperativeness.)

Step 18: You don't have to look far to see the results of this kind of thinking… or why it's so important to break up the pattern.

When I'm working to break up this thinking pattern, I repeatedly point out that **I can't help anyone directly.** I can't pretend that I can ever know **exactly** what anyone needs.

Step 19: What is real help? I think this is an extremely interesting question... and maybe you've already observed that it has a great deal of relevance to the problem of anger and violence.

Most people assume that getting angry is inevitable, and once it comes, all we can do with it is hold it in or get it out. And maybe this is true. But if it **isn't** true, this one assumption blocks us from considering another possibility: **What if the problem is that we're forming so much anger in the first place?** Once we acknowledge that this might **possibly** be the basic problem, we can look in different directions to try to get anger and violence levels down.

Step 20: I'll be offering a rationale for forming less and less anger, **and your part is to check and recheck your own observations as I go.**

Sometimes I think it's a miracle that we get along together as well as we do. That's when I see the problem of human relations as if we're trying to work a jigsaw puzzle. Maybe we're sitting at a card table trying to fit the puzzle pieces in the best places… **but every piece is moving… all the time.**

Step 21: How can we ever make plans?… know what to expect?… feel secure?… when we're all moving all the time?

#22

Instead of thinking of trying to work a jigsaw puzzle, I'll try another image. Suppose we're all a part of shifting sand, moving, slipping, sliding. Seems to me our first priority would be figuring out how to keep our own balance. If we fall down... and **don't get up fast...** we might be buried in the sand.

Step 22: I don't see much alternative to accepting that our primary job is to figure out how to function in a shifting-sand world. Is there an alternative?

But it isn't easy to keep balanced in shifting sand… **and it's no surprise that we long for more help than we can ever get.** If I think of us walking in a long parade, all going from birth to death, it's easy to see that we'd all be working to keep balanced. And we'd soon know that avoiding trouble would mean keeping our heads up and our eyes open.

Step 23: But to keep our heads up **(and this is necessary if we're to stay physically balanced)** we need to feel good about ourselves. And it's true that we'd like to **enjoy** walking in the parade. **But how do we learn to do it?**

#24

Keeping balanced shouldn't be too hard, should it? The problem is that for each of us, what we do to keep balanced, consciously and unconsciously, **is different every second.** All we can do is make our best observations... then decide what to do next... for ourselves alone. **If we think of a baby's learning to walk we can see the problem.** No words or helping hands from others can show the baby how to walk.

Step 24: We often say we want help, and maybe it's for something **only we can do for ourselves.** Is it surprising that those around us might become confused?

How many times have you desperately needed help, and you've found it at exactly the right time and place and just the way you wanted it? If we keep wanting the kind of help (in keeping balanced) that no one else can give, would it be a surprise that others are hurt by our demands and complaints... and they have trouble handling our anger **at them?**

Step 25: Maybe for this step it's enough to consider all these questions... **extra carefully.**

See what you think of this statement: Success is learning how to get along with what we can get... **willingly given...** at any one second.

Step 26: Can you think what happens to a person who doesn't believe this statement?

If your answer to that last question is that a person would be continually involved in power struggles, I think you're right. In the counseling room I see people with a lifelong belief that they need to **fight others** for what they want. **But any such power struggle is futile, as just by definition there's a winner and a loser. And what does the loser do? Wait for a chance to upset the winner.** So even the temporary winner can't enjoy the spoils of the battle… as every second is spent preparing for the next battle.

Step 27: Can you see that power struggles with others don't really end?

A big problem with power struggles is that each round takes more energy. If I throw one rock, you think you'll have to throw two (so you can get a decisive win). So I think I have to throw three. (After all, just look at what **you** did.) **In time, real problems stay on the sidelines as we each become increasingly engrossed in the power struggle itself.** The people I see in the counseling room are at an absolute dead end. **They know that continuing to fight is intolerable, yet giving up is also intolerable.**

Step 28: How can a person find an alternative to the **thinking** which creates a power-struggle trap?

#29

I suspect that everyone trapped inside a power struggle really wants out. **But in our society, how can we find an alternative?** Power struggles are everywhere, and if a person feels helpless and believes fighting is **all** that can be done **to relieve their own helplessness,** it's impossible to stop and compromise at mid-point. Belief in a "balance of power" keeps each person incessantly watching the other, ever ready to punish another's misstep. **The power struggle may seem dormant, harmless, but it's ready to burst out in an instant.**

Step 29: Can you see an alternative?

#30

If it were clear to me **exactly** how a person in the counseling room finds an alternative to their power-struggle mindset, I'd be happy to tell you about it. But since it isn't clear, what I'll do is write out, in general terms, what I tell people in the counseling room.

Step 30: Your part is to go beyond the generalities and fill in your own details.

31

Let's go back to the image of walking in a long parade, on shifting sand, with all of us trying to keep balanced. It's always risky. Others seem too ready to say that we're crazy, stupid, bad. And even when we're certain we know exactly which step to take, it sometimes turns out wrong. **If we ourselves can't ever know, for sure and in advance, exactly which step will be right for us at any one second, at least we can also be sure that no one on the sidelines can ever know.**

Step 31: Here's your question: Why are we criticizing and judging each other so much?

#32

Is it possible to really know another person and understand why they're doing what they do? I don't think so. I see us as too complicated to be understood… even by ourselves. Yet we talk and **try so hard** to get **some idea** of how another person's mind works. I suspect that the most we can ever know is about one percent.

Step 32: What I see is that we live **mostly** by guesses about nearly everything… but we tend to forget that they're only guesses. **What happens when we forget this?**

33

I think that **we want to believe** that others are **mostly** like us so we can explain their behavior by way of our own theories. So we tend to push the evidence. But the problem I see, if we truly believe that we have the power to understand others, especially those closest to us, is that **we tend to think we don't really need to listen.**

Step 33: Have you ever been convinced you knew why another person was doing something… and later found you were completely wrong?

34

Can we really talk to each other about how we're keeping our balance... at any one second? Rarely, as I think it's so complicated that we'd have to be talking all the time... and others couldn't listen very much as they'd be too busy keeping their own balance. My brain goes much faster than I can talk, anyway, so I can't really tell you what's going on with me. It's also easy to mislead you, as I can smile when I'm scared, or pose as big and tough when I feel the most helpless.

Step 34: How can we ever feel confident that we can know what's going on?

#35

Sometimes I think of our brain as a garbage heap, always in danger of being overwhelmed with incoming material. So we're busy trying to decide what to keep and what to toss. Since everything we take in has to fit somewhere, we're making decisions and shifting around that lifetime collection of bits and pieces… **every second.**

Step 35: How could we possibly know what sorting problems, what decisions, another person is working on **at any one second?** Can that person ever tell us… and do it so our garbage heap can make sense out of it?

36

I use the image of our brain as a garbage heap, with pieces shifting all the time, to repeatedly show that it's unlikely that we can ever understand another person. After all, we all have **different** pieces, **and they're constantly moving.** Wouldn't it be extremely unusual if we **could** understand another… even briefly? This is interesting, as people in the counseling room continually say, "I can't understand… I can't understand," just as if they keep **expecting** to understand.

Step 36: Can we accept that really understanding each other is probably impossible?

#37

At some point, in our incessant struggle to keep balanced, when we realize that it truly is unlikely that we'll **ever** be able to **understand** each other… or **get as much help from others as we'd like,** how do we find the courage to keep going?

Step 37: It doesn't make it any easier to find an answer to that question when we realize that **only** our own answer will work **for us.**

#38

I'll give you my answer to the question about finding courage. **We make up theories.** As we're stumbling and recovering, we find that some of our theories work to keep our courage up, and some don't. Even though our basic theories may fit with larger belief systems with well-known labels, **I'm writing about the infinite number of smaller beliefs, the theories that we're continually changing as we go.**

Step 38: What if our best theory is that we need to **wet down that shifting sand around us...** and keep it steady... so keeping balanced will be easier?

#39

Wouldn't we keep making plans and **expecting** that the shifting sand will stay our way? **(After all, look how hard we're trying to wet it down and hold it.)** I think we'd be continually disappointed... and either blame ourselves or others (who just won't cooperate enough). Or we may conclude **the problem is that we ourselves are a failure...** all because we're unable to see that wetting down that sand, and keeping it our way, **is an impossible job.**

Step 39: What happens if we continually believe we're a failure?

40

I see nothing but trouble for those who believe that they're only successful **if they get the shifting sand to stay their way.** As hard as they try, they'll stay helpless to do an impossible job. And when **helplessness** becomes intolerable, **anger** and **violence** become inevitable.

Step 40: This sequence is so clear, I wonder if you see it too. People try to convince me how justified they are to be in angry power struggles, and this is my question to you: Would it make any difference if we believe our angry power struggles are justified… if they don't work **for us… in the long run?**

#41

Instead of choosing a theory (to keep our courage up) that keeps us **trying** and **failing** to wet down the shifting sand, we might decide to try this theory: **Why not find a leader to follow, one who will show us how to survive in shifting sand?**

Step 41: What do you think the consequences would be if we truly believe that if we'll just find the right leader we can keep balanced?

42

If nothing else, we might spend our lives looking for the perfect leader. And the price we'd pay for following any leader **too much** would be our own growing **helplessness...** and increased fears of "going it alone."

Step 42: Can you see where this kind of **helplessness** inevitably leads? both for individuals and all of us as part of a larger society?

#43

What would happen if our best theory (to keep our courage up) is that we should tiptoe around so nobody will notice or criticize us? Safe in shifting sand at last? I think we'd be shoved to the sidelines of the parade and feel totally helpless. If our helplessness leads to anger and violence, **it would probably be a greater shock to ourselves than to others.**

Step 43: Have you seen an example of this?

44

Once we accept that we're in a shifting-sand world, and that stumbling and recovering is the only way we can find what works for us, **we can see that we're not bad when we try theories which won't work.** Yet we know that some of our theories work better than others, and we like to share our best ones. **But how can we tell others what will work for them if they have different shifting tidbits in their garbage heaps?**

Step 44: Maybe you see what I do, that all we can do is tell each other **what works for us...** and hope our words are clear enough that others can try our theories... **if they choose.**

45

Here's my best theory... I see our brain not only as a garbage heap, but also as a computer with the purpose of helping us keep balanced. So I'm continually getting messages, "Try this... try that." I can't know, consciously, all that's in my computer/garbage heap at any one time, or exactly why I'm making my decisions. But I choose to believe that **with whatever tidbits my garbage heap is using at any one instant, I'm made so that I'm doing the best I can just trying to keep balanced.**

Step 45: It's your part here to remind yourself that **I'm not writing about facts... but about making up a theory to try.**

46

I'm making a choice, **a choice to find out what happens** when I choose to believe that **we're all made** so we're doing the best we can… all the time… just trying to keep balanced. What's good about this theory is that it can go with me wherever I go. It's as if I take my own judge and jury with me, and I'll always know, **in advance,** that I'll be doing my best. Whenever I fall down, it's easy to find the courage to get back up, as I know that even at my best **I'm made** so I'll still stumble.

Step 46: You think this is a ridiculous theory to try?

#47

I might tell you that I did my best today, and you'd easily understand that. But what I'm writing about now, choosing to believe that **we're made** so we're all doing the best we can, all the time, means this: **We can always define what we're doing... this instant... as our best.** We're just acknowledging that we're unable to know why our computer makes each decision. And if we choose to believe **we're made** so we're always doing our best, we proceed **differently and more effectively than when we believe the opposite.**

Step 47: You're still puzzled? but it's becoming clearer?

48

A barrier to being able to accept this belief, for some people, is that they think they'd never make any progress if they continually pronounced themselves as doing their best all the time. This is interesting, as many people have a tendency to believe that self-criticism is what keeps us moving ahead. Maybe that's so. **But what I see is that when we accept ourselves as doing our best all the time, our stress and strain level goes way down.** And we begin to make **better** decisions, not worse.

Step 48: Does this fit enough with your experience that it's making sense... yet?

49

What I'm suggesting is that there really is a way to see the world so we aren't so suspicious and hostile. Because suspicion and hostility feed on themselves, **in that context** we think that **all** we can do is strike back at each other. As we intensify our power struggles, constantly fighting others and defending ourselves, it's difficult to label what we're doing as our best. In fact, we well may hate ourselves.

Step 49: We're back to the old question again. **How can we move from a power-struggle lifestyle to one of cooperation?**

50

People in the counseling room often tell me that there's something wrong with them, maybe something's missing. It's as if they see their anger as a monster inside them, always ready to jump out and embarrass them. As I listen, I hear the progression of thinking which has led them to where they are: painfully engrossed in trying to find what's wrong with them… and desperately fighting to keep the monster of their anger out of sight.

Step 50: Maybe you'll remember that the evidence that something's wrong is their failure to get through to others and get more help. **Do you too see this as tragic?**

51

The way I see it, when we see ourselves as bad (wrong, inadequate...), **that judgment alone contaminates every step we take.** Instead of being able to go ahead with confidence, we keep doubling back, obsessed with getting what we can't get... in order to make ourselves all right (by our own definition... as we can't see that we're **already** doing our best).

Step 51: Can you see why people entering the counseling room say they're at a dead end? They know they're trying as hard as they can, so the **only** thing they know to do, **try harder,** has become impossible.

52

When we think we're bad (wrong, inadequate…), we're afraid that we really aren't walking at the same parade level as others. **If we believe we're six inches below, for example, then every second must be a fight to show that we belong at least up to parade level.** This means endless power struggles to get more help (maybe **special** treatment) in order to prove to everyone that we're where we ought to be. But the more we're denied our claims to specialness, the more painful it is to keep trying.

Step 52: Can you see how repeating this pattern may lead to being unable to find the courage to get up at all?

53

One of the most interesting things I've learned in the counseling room is this: Power struggles (attempts to get what isn't there) are often waged not only by way of anger, but with **niceness.**

Step 53: Maybe this isn't surprising to you. And maybe you easily see how our goal (to get more help) might be the same, whether we use anger or niceness. **But this point is so important, I hope you'll pause here and consider it very carefully.**

54

What do you think it would be like to believe each day that if we'll just be nicer we can get the help we believe we have to have? **And then find each day that we still can't be nice enough?** From this position, it's too difficult to see that what's wanted is **impossible** to get **(as others have to put keeping their own balance first)**. And we make things worse when we believe that **we ourselves must be a failure** because our niceness is failing.

Step 54: Can you see where this pattern leads?

55

You can probably see that the pattern I've just described often leads to helplessness and anger... and then violence. In the counseling room, I see people who have done all kinds of battering of others, all the way to committing murder. And a common belief for each person is that **they ought to be able to be nice enough to get the help they crave.**

Step 55: Maybe, as you're checking and rechecking your own observations, you aren't surprised that this is a common belief with those who come in for counseling.

#56

Sifting through my thousands of hours listening in the counseling room, I was most surprised to reach the **following conclusion: I suspect that all anger (yes, all anger) comes from disappointment and confusion when our niceness never seems to be enough (to get the longed-for help and cooperation which always stays just out of reach).**

Step 56: It's your turn to do even more thinking. What do you see?

57

It was very difficult for me to believe, at first, that the most angry people I see are really trying to be nicer, more helpful and more pleasing. [For an in-depth look at angry pleasers, you'll find a 30-page supplement (full-sized pages) in both **SHAKE THE ANGER HABIT!** (1990 revised edition) and **GETTING THROUGH TO OTHERS WITHOUT ANGER** (1994).]

Step 57: Originally I talked and wrote about an anger trap, and then it became an anger/power-struggle trap. I think you can now see why I sometimes call it an **angry-pleaser**/power-struggle trap.

#58

Once a would-be pleaser gets angry and maybe violent, because their attempts to get what they want have failed, everything gets worse. In addition to feeling self-hate ("Am I a monster of some kind?... that's just not like me."), the anger and violence, as usual, will boomerang.

Step 58: From the turmoil inside the trap, it's like a broken record stuck with just one thought: "If only I could get this... or that... **then** I'd be all right... If only I could get this... or that... **then** I'd be all right." **Can you see how this theory leads to ever-increasing pain?**

#59

Maybe we'll say something like this: **"If only I could get you to understand how important this is to me..."** The assumption is that if we could just get through and get the other to understand, **then** we'd get help. Believing this means that we feel forced to keep trying to get through. Maybe we have to talk louder? faster? oftener? more eloquently? But nothing is working, as others probably resent our attempts to control them and they're moving away.

Step 59: I call anger a knife to the heart... **as we use it in a desperate attempt to get through** (and get help). Can you see that this is where violence originates?

#60

How do we know when we're asking too much of each other? Here's one way of thinking about an answer to that question. If life is a game of cards, we're all wild cards (as we're all able to play any place). By imagining a playing card standing up on end, moving in a parade, **it's easy to see how fragile our balance would be.**

Step 60: At any one minute I don't think we can ever look at another person and know, for sure, if the other can help us or not. **Can you see how we hurt each other by expecting what isn't available?**

61

Getting through to each other doesn't always mean trying to get the help we want from each other. **I also see getting through as being able to get a fair hearing.** I think that knowing how to get through to each other **without anger** (in order to get a fair hearing) is what helps us feel powerful, **the exact opposite of the helplessness which triggers anger and violence.**

Step 61: See if you agree: **Maybe we help others the most by listening while they sort out their own garbage heap... and they get a fair hearing from us.** And maybe others are most willing to give us a fair hearing **after** we've listened to them first.

62

Being able to listen and give each other the opportunity to get a fair hearing, I believe, is absolutely **essential** if we're to feel good about ourselves and others. **When I look at society's anger, I don't think we'll be able to get the tension down unless we recognize the importance of really listening to each other.** And we can't listen if we're endlessly defensive and engaged in hostile power struggles... or hiding our heads in the sand.

Step 62: Maybe you see that our first priority may be getting ourselves in shape **so we can listen. That's what this book is about.**

63

As a talkshow guest discussing anger and violence, I'm often asked what I see ahead. Of course I don't know, but I respond that **the harder we make it to get through to each other to get a fair hearing, the more problems we'll have with anger and violence.**

Step 63: Probably you can see that what gets in the way of our giving each other a fair hearing is our own anger (our non-acceptance of each other). **And the opposite is being able to see that we don't deserve each other's anger...** as we're all doing the best we can... all the time... just trying to keep our balance.

64

In earlier books I included a sketch to summarize the thinking behind what I call the anger habit. And you'll see the same sketch on the next page. **I'm using it here for a review, and I think the pages which follow clearly show how to break the habit of forming so much anger.**

Step 64: Can you see how the thinking I've been describing can be called a habit? And that it's a habit which keeps us stuck in the anger trap?

Step 65:
The entrance to the trap is at the top. After you examine the sketch, you may want to note the page number so you can refer to it later.

FAULTY OBSERVATIONS

FAULTY EXPECTATIONS

CATCH 22

ISOLATION

THE ANGER TRAP

HURT

HELPLESSNESS

MIXED FEELINGS

ANGER

FAULTY OBSERVATIONS: If we don't see the shifting sand, and all of us as wild cards teetering along in the parade, we keep thinking that the world ought to be different (more able to help us keep balanced). **But we don't set out to become engrossed in angry power struggles to get what we think we have to have.** Instead, our FAULTY OBSERVATIONS lead us to believe that the help we want ought to come to us **willingly given.**

Step 66: Because we're focusing so much on what's missing, **you can probably see that we're blinded to what's right in our lives... maybe including what others are doing for us... willingly.**

67

FAULTY EXPECTATIONS: As we start to go around inside the trap, we soon reach **FAULTY EXPECTATIONS**. After all, look how hard we're trying. Won't we be rewarded soon? If we're unaware of the shifting sand and that we're all doing the best we can to keep balanced at this minute, our **FAULTY EXPECTATIONS** don't seem faulty to us. Maybe we just need more patience and **then** we'll get what we expect?

Step 67: How can anything but **FAULTY EXPECTATIONS** come from **FAULTY OBSERVATIONS?**

68

HURT: We keep feeling HURT when we're expecting what isn't there **(the help, cooperation, appreciation... the signs of others' caring which we want willingly given).** Probably we truly believe that our **only** reaction to disappointment ought to be HURT, and the HURT seems to come suddenly... out of the air... and it grabs us.

Step 68: The sequence seems awfully clear, from FAULTY OBSERVATIONS to FAULTY EXPECTATIONS and then to HURT. It helps me (and you too?) to see that we can feel HURT any time we want to... **any time we believe the shifting sand ought to be more cooperative.**

69

TURN-OFF POINT: We can get out of the trap between FAULTY EXPECTATIONS and HURT. Every time **(and I do mean every time)** we don't get what we expect, **we can ask ourselves this question:** What is wrong with **my** expectations that I keep expecting **this** and getting **that?** Once we've asked ourselves that question, we're no longer stuck in trying to get **others** to be the way we want them to be. We've simply walked out of the trap and into the moving parade. **Now we're rechecking and correcting our own** FAULTY OBSERVATIONS.

Step 69: With our eyes open, we can see that **everything looks different** than when we were half-blinded with HURT.

70

HELPLESSNESS: If we don't walk out of the trap and into the parade, we'll walk with our heads down and our eyes half closed. It's as if we're on a greased slide, as every HURT leads to the next. From inside the trap, trying **harder and oftener** to make things better means we just slide downhill faster.

Step 70: HELPLESSNESS is intolerable, and we'll do nearly anything to relieve it... and that includes doing things which are certain to hurt us later. You can see that it's our **total desperation** (when we find our niceness isn't enough to force those bad guys to help us so we can feel better) **that compels us to use anger and violence.**

71

ANGER AND VIOLENCE: Once we get angry, even though we never act on it directly, I think we hurt ourselves. But when we do act, and begin telling others that we don't like what they're doing **and that they really ought to be different,** we're in a losing position. Others just don't accept our belief that we know better **than they do** what **they** should be doing to keep their balance at any one minute.

Step 71: You can make your own list of the results of the kind of thinking which begins with **FAULTY OBSERVATIONS,** the kind of thinking which is repeatedly used to justify forming anger.

72

MIXED FEELINGS: Once we've exploded in anger and maybe violence, our biggest problem is knowing, deep inside, that it didn't work. We wanted help (cooperation, appreciation), but we wanted it given willingly. **Yet it's impossible to get anything willingly given by way of anger. So nothing we get feels good as it's always tainted by doubts. We can't tell if it was given because of others' caring... or because of their fear of our anger.**

Step 72: You can see the confusion and despair in recognizing that our angry power struggles will always be failing.

73

ISOLATION, #1: As far as I can tell, each person who comes into the counseling room is at the point of **ISOLATION**. And it doesn't matter whether they have isolated themselves (for fear of hurting others) or others have isolated them (also out of fear). If their self-anger (guilt) is high enough, they may be suicidal.

Step 73: Maybe you too have been misled by such a person's exaggerated claims of success: **"I really fixed 'em… they'll never mess with me again."** But how many times can a person say that **before becoming totally isolated by their anger?**

74

ISOLATION, **#2:** The pain and possibility of violence becomes more intense the longer a person is isolated. The trap spins faster each time we tell ourselves that we really ought to be getting more help (cooperation, appreciation) **if we'll just try hard enough.** Those around us are increasingly confused as **we're nice one minute and maybe mean the next.** But we feel forced to continue to fight so we can finally get up to parade level. **Yet each failure increases our terror of even more isolation.**

Step 74: Maybe you can make a list of the words used to describe a person at this point: **bizarre, erratic, a loner...**

75

ISOLATION, **#3**: It's certain that we'll continue to push others away… even those who want to help us. We're so terrified that there's something terribly wrong with us (just look at the way people are pulling away) that we're vowing each day to be nicer and nicer and nicer. **In this state, even one word of criticism is intolerable… and almost certain to provoke violence.**

Step 75: Can you see how this works? and everything moves towards keeping us even more isolated?

76

ISOLATION, **#4:** Instead of using alcohol, drugs, (or even suicide) to avoid the terrors of increasing isolation, maybe we'll just go numb and stay depressed. When every breath carries the risk that we'll say the wrong thing, or hear even a **hint** of criticism, it seems that the less we do and say the better.

Step 76: You can probably see that we're getting the opposite of what we want... again. **Just because we've dampened down our feelings to avoid the risks of talking and listening, our FAULTY OBSERVATIONS are becoming more faulty than ever.** ("Things really ought to be more the way I think they ought to be.")

77

ISOLATION, #5: You probably know the theory that when we're numb (depressed), it's because we're not getting our anger out enough. And in our society, it usually doesn't occur to us that the problem might be **our thinking pattern** which keeps us forming anger in the first place. **When we're already depressed and isolated by our anger, would it help to believe that we really should be telling others, more often, that we're angry at them?**

Step 77: Or do you think it would be better to find that we don't have to make FAULTY OBSERVATIONS and justify anger and keep ourselves isolated?

78

ISOLATION, **#6:** Probably you can see that we'll be further isolated if we truly believe that **old buried anger is our problem,** and we need to get it out **(in addition to today's anger).** What I find is that when we break the anger habit **today,** the old anger seems to disappear. Once we see that we really are doing the best we can, and we're enjoying a lifestyle in which others are coming closer, **we don't need to find theories to explain our pain and isolation.**

Step 78: We can resurrect the old anger if we want to, **but you can see that we'd have to get back into the anger trap to find it.**

79

CATCH **22:** This is the last point on the angry-pleaser/power-struggle trap before we whirl around again **(and probably faster, as the course is so familiar).** CATCH **22** indicates the dilemma. We can't make better observations and find out what the world is really like **when we're isolated.** We can't correct our FAULTY OBSERVATIONS when others are unwilling to come close and tell us the truth… as they're too afraid of our anger and unpredictable behavior.

Step 79: Can you see that finding our way out of the anger trap on our own, **from this position, would be extremely difficult?**

#80

After people break out of the trap, they often tell me that it happens something like this. At first, when they get angry, it may be days before they remind themselves that we're all doing the best we can all the time… **and they recheck their observations with this in mind.** Then each time they get angry, the faster they remember. **The anguish caused by their anger shrinks to just a few seconds… then to practically nothing.** "It's exciting," they tell me, "I can't believe the difference."

Step 80: When a person finds **how** to get out of the trap, just **one** time, you can see that from there on, **it's just a choice**… to stay inside or to get out.

81

When I use my experience inside the counseling room as a guide to seeing what's going on in our society, it appears that our society's helplessness stems from the same root as individual helplessness: As a society, we're trying too hard, just in **bigger and more dramatic** ways, to force others **to make our lives easier** (cooperate and do what we want them to do). Yet it's easy to predict that our **bigger and more dramatic** methods of using force will continue to provoke **bigger and more dramatic** responses.

Step 81: You can see that more thinking is needed about our **problem-solving style itself.**

82

Recently I saw a parked car with two bumper stickers:
AN ARMED SOCIETY IS A POLITE SOCIETY and **PEACE THROUGH FIREPOWER.** I moved away, fast, as I didn't feel safe around that car. **Are we really safer, or in more danger, when we try to control each other by force?**

Step 82: Obviously some people's computer/garbage heaps come up with one answer to this question... and others the opposite. And nothing is gained by each faction pushing the other to appreciate **their** observations and reach **their** conclusions. How do **you** think we can be safer with each other?

83

The childhood game of cops and robbers seems to be escalating, and in some areas prison populations are growing faster than the general population. Maybe we'll reach the point at which fifty percent of us are behind bars. Will we be any safer then? Seventy-five percent? Can real safety **ever** be achieved by controlling others by force?

Step 83: As individuals **get trapped** in the only lifestyle they know (one of win-lose problem solving), do you suppose the same thing is true in our society? And the **only** reason we can't seek an alternative to win-lose is that **we can't believe that one exists?**

#84

I suspect that you too have plenty of evidence that the answer to the last question is yes. Many times, when talking to others about the escalating cops and robbers game, I'll hear these exact words: "But we all know that more law enforcement isn't the answer... but right now we don't have any other choice." **(This is just one example of a society-approved power struggle in which both groups fan fears of the other... and there never seems to be a good place to stop.)**

Step 84: What do **you** see ahead with cops and robbers... or any other society-approved power struggle?

85

I think we're in danger of seeing our cops and robbers game come to a crashing halt. When people who are trapped in a power-struggle mindset come into the counseling room, **they've waited until their own resources are totally exhausted.** I wonder. Does that mean that for our society, we won't seek an alternative to our current problem-solving methods until we're forced to... **when our resources are totally exhausted?**

Step 85: Maybe finding an alternative to unending power struggles begins to look better... and better... and better.

86

Here's another example of a pending power-struggle crash. We'll say a couple is fighting, and this is the image I get. It's as if both of them are hanging onto the edge of a cliff, clinging by their fingernails, and there's a deep canyon below. As they're hanging on for their life, **each is blaming the other for not lending a hand.**

Step 86: What is the inevitable result if we continue to expect help that isn't available? Don't we weaken each other by our demands and complaints... and hasten our mutual downfall?

87

I suspect that **every** complaint and **every** power struggle adds to our society's tensions and troubles. And I'm including the struggles so small they don't show to the outside world, all the way to those in today's headlines. **How do we live in a climate of so much tension?**

Step 87: Whenever it becomes intolerable we scramble for safety. And you can probably make a long list of the ways we scramble… **and list some advantages and disadvantages of each… for ourselves as well as for society.**

#88

One way we're trying to find safety, **and we hurt ourselves instead**, is by focusing on the **triggers** for anger and violence **(as if the triggers are the causes).** Then we conclude that if only we can **"fix" enough of the triggers,** and do it fast enough, **then** we'll be safe.

Step 88: Maybe we especially like this conclusion, as it keeps us busy and not **too overwhelmed** by helplessness. And I'm certain we're relieving much misery with our "fixing." **But I wonder if you can see how too much focus on triggers for anger and violence... hurts us in the long run?**

89

What I see is that working so hard to "fix" the triggers for anger and violence means that we miss what may be much more important: We don't even see the **possibility** that our problems may stem from **a thinking pattern which repeatedly justifies forming anger** (not from each individual incident which we say causes anger).

Step 89: You probably know at least one person who is often angry, and you've seen that the triggers for that person's anger are sometimes "fixed." But after each "fixing," what did you see? **Didn't that person just shift the focus of their anger to something else?**

90

What is it that we can do… **that really works…** to make things better? It's obvious that tensions will be decreased when we're more able to be supportive instead of tearing each other apart. And it's clear to me that we'll be able to be more supportive when our thinking is such that we see others as doing their best… **and if we also know how to give support.**

Step 90: What I've found is that many people believe they're being supportive when they aren't. Since **knowing how to be supportive** is so crucial to our getting society's anger and violence down, here's your question: **What is it we do that shows real support?**

#91

I think we give support to each other by **listening.** It's being listened to which helps us feel that we're **powerful,** able to get through to others, and maybe **valued**, **appreciated** and **respected**. And I think it takes realizing how desperately **we ourselves** want to be listened to that helps us see that **others probably want the same.**

Step 91: It's defensiveness and fear of what we'll hear that blocks our ability to listen and support each other. But we can easily get beyond our defensiveness when we remind ourselves that we're truly doing the best we can… all the time.

#92

I'm thinking now about the **aloneness** we all share, the **genuine aloneness** we feel walking in a parade in which every step is risky. To me, enjoying the walking means remembering **at each step** to make the best of whatever we have. Then we're continually staying balanced and looking ahead… **and others are willing to come close.**

Step 92: You can see how important it is to us that others are willing to come close, as then we can compare notes about our balance-keeping. **I think this is what makes our genuine aloneness tolerable.**

#93

Maybe the best reason for keeping our balance is that if we don't **we'll be scaring people away...** and feeling even more alone than ever. Just because we're off balance (and certain that we can't keep balanced unless we get some kind of help), others resist our demands. **Then our panic increases as we see them moving away.**

Step 93: Out of such panic you can see why someone may say this: "I'll kill you if you leave me." Or instead, the person may say, "I'll kill myself if you leave me."

94

The way I see it, our success and pleasure in walking in the parade depends on our ability to accept what comes... **but that doesn't mean being passive.** It means, instead, being alert and being balanced... as this is the best starting place for whatever we're doing at each second... **if we want to be effective.**

Step 94: Accepting this starting place doesn't mean that we always like it. But you probably can agree that it's wiser to **acknowledge the limits of what we have to work with at any one second...** rather than stay unbalanced because we're reaching for what's out of reach.

95

You probably know it's not easy to be accepting of each other… at all times. **What helps, I think, is to realize how much we ourselves, at a deep level, want to be accepted exactly as we are at each minute.**

Step 95: But have you ever noticed how stingy we tend to be in giving others the same kind of acceptance that we want for ourselves?

It's not easy to be accepting **when another person's anger is directed at us.** I think it helps to see that the angry person is whirling around inside **their own trap,** and it's best if we don't try to **help** them or **change** them or **plead guilty to "badness."** By making keeping our own balance our first priority, we can sense the desperate helplessness of a person who may be saying something like this: "Nothing I ever do is right... so why try?"

Step 96: Would it help to get mad when a person is saying that?... or use force, or logical arguments, to try to persuade that person to see things differently?

#97

After we've felt someone's anger at us, what do we say? I'm sure you know that nothing may be "right" at that time. Yet anything we say (maybe much later) will come out better if we're balanced ourselves... **and if we don't make matters worse by defending our supposed badness.**

Step 97: Can you see that whatever we say at the time of the outburst will probably **cause more confusion** for the person whirling around in their own anger trap... frantically trying to sort out their own anguish?

#98

After an angry outburst, **I've come to believe that the angry person probably feels far worse than the person who was the target of the anger.** What I see is that we're living in a society made up of millions of such people, **unwillingly trapped** in angry power struggles and feeling **forced** to fight others who are also **unwillingly trapped** in angry power struggles.

Step 98: It's no wonder that so many of us are hiding our heads in the sand and hoping the inevitable firestorms of anger will go somewhere else. **Since you've read this far, my guess is that you too believe that we're not completely helpless.**

99

I think the biggest favor we can do for each other is to learn how to put out **our own** brushfires of anger (even if they're only tiny ones). That means **more** of us can become **more** accepting and **more** able to listen to each other… so we can see **more** tension go down around us.

Step 99: Maybe you're surprised to find where all these steps have led? **And maybe you've been surprised to find that your own anger level has been going down as you've been reading? And maybe you deserve congratulations?**

100

You can probably guess that others will be grateful when you share what you've learned… and maybe they too will find that they don't have to be **forming so much anger… and scaring others away.** Maybe you're planning to pass this book around?… or donate it to a library?… or you'll come up with more and better ideas?

Step 100: Do you think that enough of us… can cut the anguish caused by **our own anger** fast enough… that we can make a noticeable difference in our society's anger level? **Shall we find out?**

ORDER FORM — THE BOOKERY PUBLISHING CO.

❖ Order by phone, fax or mail. Full refund if not satisfied ❖

6899 Riata Dr. Redding, CA 96002-(916) 365-8068-Fax (916) 365-8082

____ 100 THINGS WE CAN DO ABOUT ANGER & VIOLENCE $ _____
(1994, DOTY) ISBN 0-930822-18-8, $9.95

____ (Audio cassette) 100 THINGS WE CAN DO ABOUT ANGER $ _____
& VIOLENCE ISBN 0-930822-20-X, $19.95

____ GETTING THROUGH TO OTHERS WITHOUT ANGER $ _____
(1994, Doty) ISBN 0-930822-17-X, $11.95

____ (Audio cassette) GETTING THROUGH TO OTHERS $ _____
WITHOUT ANGER ISBN 0-930822-19-6, $24.95

____ SHAKE THE ANGER HABIT! (1990, Doty/Rooney) $ _____
ISBN 0-930822-10-2, $11.95

____ (Audio cassette) SHAKE THE ANGER HABIT! $ _____
ISBN 0-930822-12-9, $24.95

____ THE ANGER PUZZLE (1986, Doty/Rooney) $ _____
ISBN 0-930822-07-2 $8.95

____ BREAK THE ANGER TRAP (1985, Doty) $ _____
ISBN 0-930822-06-4, $8.95

____ MARRIAGE INSURANCE (1978, Doty) (a series of $ _____
communication exercises for two people to use together)
ISBN 0-930822-01-3 $8.95

Continued ☞